I0481306

PENNY STOCKS

The Beginner's Guide to Building
Massive Wealth

ALAN D. RICE

PUBLISHED BY: Alan D. Rice

Copyright © 2016 All rights reserved.

No part of this publication may be copied, reproduced in any format, by any means, electronic or otherwise, without prior consent from the copyright owner and publisher of this book.

Table of Contents

INTRODUCTION

I want to thank you and congratulate you for downloading *Penny Stocks: The Beginner's Guide to Building Massive Wealth.* This book is intended for the beginner investor seeking to make money through the stock market by trading penny stocks. This book will walk you through all the basics of penny stocks, explaining clearly and succinctly exactly how they function and why they are an effective method of gaining profit through the stock market.

As an individual investor, you are stepping into a market where you can truly compete. The costs for entry are relatively low, and the swings in stock are large enough that you can truly make a great profit. Penny stocks offer the individual investor an unparalleled level of freedom in terms of investment, and the styles of trading that can be practiced on penny stocks are on par with the styles that are conducive to success on large exchanges. I come to you now with the tips and strategies that I have learned and how to apply these strategies to making a profit on penny stocks. Within my first year I was able to clear six figures, and I believe the same can be said for any individual with the gumption and drive to succeed in the market. Over the course of the following chapters I will explain everything you need to know about penny stocks. Whether you are a veteran investor in other markets, or are completely new to the field, I aim to illustrate all of the essential aspects of penny stocks so that you have the requisite knowledge to get ahead.

It's time to take a chance, one based on the tools and knowledge that have helped me succeed in the market. The capital requirements are low, the rewards are large, and the ability to succeed is entirely determined by your desire to make a great profit. Continue reading and soon you will have the tools to succeed in penny stocks, clearing the way to financial freedom and giving you the ability to provide a better future for you and your family.

I wish you the best of luck!

Alan D. Rice

———

CHAPTER 1

UNDERSTANDING PENNY STOCKS

Penny Stock Essentials

Penny stocks receive their namesake from their very low cost per share. It is a common misconception that all penny stocks trade at under just a dollar. While referred to as 'penny stocks', the actual definition is a bit more complicated. They are stocks for publically listed companies that require far less review to be listed on exchanges, and they specifically must be trading at a value of less than five dollars per share, as defined by the Securities and Exchange Commission.

What penny stocks offer is very different from what you will find on more traditional exchanges like the

NASDAQ and Dow Jones Industrial. They are companies that are just starting out, and typically have not finalized their business model. Typically, these companies focus on good rather than services, and their products are not yet at the point where they are ready to be sold. That is, the companies that often have issued penny stock are working on the development of a product and are seeking investment from outside investors such as yourself. To understand why these companies are seeking investment at all, you must first familiarize yourself with the concept of market capitalization. Market capitalization is a very simple mathematical formula, but the end result represents a number that determines the very real ability for a company to take out loans.

Let's say for example that the total number of outstanding shares of a company rests at one thousand. The outstanding shares represent the total number of shares that have been sold or are being held by the company. Suppose that each share is being sold for one dollar. This would put the total market cap for this fictional company at one thousand dollars. The formula therefore for market capitalization is the total number of outstanding shares multiplied by the average price per share. Once you have determined the market capitalization for a company, you can then assume that this is the total amount that outside investors would be willing to lend to that company. In our example, the total amount that an outside firm would be willing to lend is one thousand dollars.

This amount actually makes perfect sense if you think about what the stock value represents; it is the total amount of investments made by investors that are not guaranteed their money back, but more importantly it represents the total interest that public investors have in a company. You will notice that the market capitalization for very large companies, think on the scale of Starbucks or Apple, have market caps in the billions of dollars. They can borrow against what investors see as a steady investment due to public investors believing that the company holds at least this value. In real terms, if the stock were to be made liquid, that is if all of the stock was sold for cash, then private investors would be able to be paid back.

It's important to note the fundamental difference between penny stocks and stocks listed on larger exchanges. Take for instance Apple and what it means to own Apple stock. You are investing in Apple and expanding their market capitalization; that is, you are expanding the amount of money that Apple can borrow to expand their inventory or further product research. Penny stocks offer the same type of investment, but they will immediately be borrowing against their market capitalization. While Apple sells stock, the truth is that they really don't need investors in the same way that penny stocks do. Apple does not need to borrow money because they have a large amount of cash on hand, but for the purpose of producing their products they often use loaned money to finalize shipments and research new products.

They use money that is on loan because there is no reason not to. It essence, it is safer to gable with someone else's money than their own. The interesting thing about how market capitalization fits into larger companies is that aside from already having money on hand, they are also very far along in terms of their total number of assets and their product line. Take for instance if Apple's stock were to dramatically decrease. For purposes of illustrating this point, suppose that the stock value falls all the way down to fifty cents, a completely unrealistic situation that would take literally decades of poor management and product failures. Even when the stock price falls to this incredibly low value, Apple would still have lots of inventory to sell.

Think about all of the iPads, iPhones, Macs and other products that Apple sells. It is not as if all of these assets would disappear. The point is that Apple does not need a large amount of money to develop their first product or build their infrastructure of stores around the United States and the world. These are assets that they already have, and fixed assets that are not going anywhere. Furthermore, the cost of researching a *new* MacBook is far less than the cost of researching the *first* MacBook. The idea I want you to walk away from here is that penny stock companies are often on the first step of their business model that precedes having any sort of product that is ready for the consumer, but also that the research and development of this first product is always going to cost more than further revisions.

For a penny stock company, it means that if they are able to get their first product out the door, and even if it only has minimal success, they will be able to iterate on this product with minimal further investment. In essence, the stock becomes safer after they have shipped their first product. Penny stocks become more stable therefore the further a company is into their business model, and this is not necessary tied to the age of the company.

The reason why I want to stress the importance of market capitalization comes down to liquidity and your ability to sell stock in the future. The key to making the best picks for penny stocks comes down to deciding on companies where you will be able to realize profit because they are in existence for long enough that you are able to sell stock. While this might sound like a scary idea, by the completion of this book you will have the skills to make the right picks. Market capitalization does not only determine the total amount that company can borrow against, but also shows how valuable a stock is. This becomes important for us as we trade stock because if a stock's value were to suddenly rise, this does us no good as investors if we are unable to sell the stock.

In general, a higher market capitalization equals a greater ability to sell stock. Since this is such an important concept, this will be explained in more detail in chapter six. It is essential that you are picking companies that have the proper levels of market capitalization so that you are able to move stock and make a profit on your investments.

There is one last aspect of penny stocks that I want to focus on. This is essentially the last basic principle and the last piece of essential knowledge that you will need: there are for more companies that trade on penny stock exchanges than there are trading on traditional exchanges. This is true for a variety of reasons, ranging from the cost to entry to the realistic nature of how may companies are able to compete in a single market. The ability for a company to compete in a field depends on how many immediate competitors that they have. You have to take into account that penny stock companies are trying to reach a large market, which is why they list themselves at all on any sort of exchange for public investment. They are seeking to have a national or global reach. A company that specializes in a service that is localized, for instance a cleaning company, does not require the same type of investment that penny stock companies are looking for.

A cleaning company has many competitors but the only ones that pose any sort of competition are the ones in the immediate area. A cleaning company from New York cannot clean houses and hotels in California for instance. Penny stock companies therefore have to be extremely aware of their competition because their competition exists on a world stage. The types of products that penny stock companies are developing can be sold to anyone, anywhere, and so while the market is larger, so is the ultimate pool for competition. What this means for investors like us is that we *too* have to take into account all of the competition that exist for the companies that we invest in. This is actually not a major concern for traders working on larger exchanges for a reason unique to large exchanges; competition in competing fields is simply not as common.

Take for instance search engines, and how many major search engines are traded on traditional stock exchanges. There are Yahoo, Google and Bing. Of these three major search engines, only one company has a strong focus on searches. Yahoo does not really compete with Google or Bing because they offer a variety of services outside of being a search engine. They offer email, news and chat services. Bing is not a company of and by itself; it is a part of Microsoft and exists more for the purpose of furthering Microsoft's interests rather than the interests of Bing itself. Then there is Google; Google is actually the only real search engine being traded on major exchanges in the US. The importance of this concept is that you do not find a lot of competition among similar services on large exchanges.

For an investor, what this means is that if they like the concept of 'search engines' for investment, they don't really have a choice of which company to invest in. This is far different reality on penny stock exchanges where you will find many companies that offer near identical services. This is where market capitalization becomes so handy in knowing whom to invest in, along with other strategies that I will be focusing on later. You can't simply bet on a concept; you actually have to bet on who is going to be able to execute that concept and succeed.

Over the course of the following chapters you will learn the strategies and skills necessary to make the right choices for which penny stocks to invest in, but as a summary for the essential knowledge that you need to know as you read the rest of the material, let's review: penny stocks are stocks have a relatively low cost per share, always trading at a value of less than five dollars per share. Companies that trade as penny stocks often have relatively low market capitalization, and market capitalization is essential for your ability to move shares in the future. Penny stocks exist for companies that have typically yet to release a product and are seeking investment for research, marketing the practicality of shipping their released product to stores. Penny stocks often compete directly with each other in their own sector of the economy, and they are trying to reach the appeal of markets on the scale of nations, not small communities or even individual states.

Why Do Companies Trade on Penny Stock Exchanges?

There is an essential question about penny stocks that needs to be answered: why do companies decide to list themselves on penny stock exchanges? The simple answer is that they often have no other choice, but that doesn't get at the crux for why there are so many companies that decide to list themselves and sell shares for such low prices. The answer to this question is a key point of understanding the types of companies that you will be interacting with and the types of people that run the companies that trade on the major penny stock exchanges.

We live in an age where capital flows more freely than ever before. It is easier for a company to get a loan to make a product in 2017 than at any time in history; this is just a matter of fact. What penny stock companies are trying to do is a bit unique however, in that they are trying to have wide appeal to entire nations or the globe as a whole, while at the same time typically selling a more traditional product. The companies that are you gong to be interacting with are often not software related, and the one's that are typically not worth investing in. Think about the major news stories that you've heard over the last few years relating to social media and large tech companies that have had successful initial public offerings (IPOs) or have been purchased by the large companies within their sector.

Starting with the Facebook IPO, there was an explosion in capital flowing to these tech based companies that often have no business plan, or untenable business plans. Twitter is a prime example of this. It is a company that has a healthy stock, even though it has recently been on the decline, but has absolutely no ability to make a profit, and can just barely keep up with the infrastructure costs of running the company. There are a handful of other tech companies that fall into this category, such as *Groupon.* I want to stress this idea because of how successful these companies have been at garnering investment; it leaves one to wonder why any company would need to be listed as a penny stock and might still be a company worth investing in.

The key differentiator between companies that list on penny stock exchanges and the companies that have quickly expanded and gained lots of capital like Twitter is in both the space that they compete, and how outside investors like to judge the potential value of companies. I have done lots of research about companies that little to no chance of making a profit in the next five or ten years, but what is often the deciding factor in whether or not an investment is made is how many 'users' that company is able to garner. Twitter is only as successful as it is because so many people use it. It doesn't matter that the company is being held up by outside investment and shareholders. As long as investors continue to make investment based on how many users a company can gain, it will make sense for Twitter to not be all too concerned about making a viable business plan for the future; they simply do not need to.

Compare this to penny stock companies and you will see a vast difference. With penny stock companies, they are often making products that have defined business plans, or products or services that customers actually need to pay for. In a twisted and perverse sort of way, their desire to make a more traditional product and create a viable business plan for long into the future has destined them to never be able to gain as much investment as a tech company that simply gains a lot of users but has no way to monetize that user base. What you need to be looking for in penny stock companies therefore is far more traditional than how large firms view tech based companies; you need to be on the lookout for products that can actually succeed, or at least have a good enough sounding idea and well thought out business plan that they will be able to attract investment.

CHAPTER 2

FINDING YOUR PREFERRED METHOD OF TRADING

Different Trading Styles and Capital Requirements

There are several different trading styles that you can emulate, and your own style is likely to end up combining a variety of different trading styles. The type of style that you adopt is going to depend on what you naturally gravitate to, as in which you prefer and enjoy doing, but is also a function of the amount of time that you have to dedicate to that style of trading. Day trading for example requires an immense amount of time in set chunks that can range between six and ten hours. Value traders on the other hand can dedicate thirty minutes to an hour each night and find that they can make a decent amount of profit. Most importantly about the style of trading that you adopt is going to be how investments are made and the size of those investments.

Day traders see their balance sheets at the end of each day, and in more rare cases at the end of each week. Value traders might not know the true result of their trades until months down the line. The size of your trades is also going to be dependent on your trading style. Value traders make some of the largest investments into individual companies, whereas day traders will have the smallest investments. I suggest that you try each style and find which one you like the most, and which ones you are naturally talented at. I make most of my money through day trading, but my preferred method of making investments is value trading. In the following chapters, you will learn about each style, the time investment required, and how a typical day can flow with each style. As you are reading, think about how you would fit into each style; you will almost certainly have some idea of which trading method is most suitable to your style, routine and capital requirements.

It's also worth noting that these styles of trading can be practiced on pretty much any exchange or place where trades take place instantaneously or close to instantaneously. Some styles of trading are more conducive to certain markets than others. For example, the buy and hold strategy works far better on the FOREX and traditional stock exchanges than it does on penny stocks. Day trading works best on FOREX markets, etc. As I detail each trading style I will walk you through how much money you will want to invest in each trade, but there are also general rules about how much money you should allocate to any individual trade as well.

The golden rule is that you should be investing somewhere between five to ten percent of your investment fund at most in any single trade. For example, if your total trading fund is one thousand dollars, this means that the most you should be risking on any single trade is between fifty and one hundred dollars. I highly suggest that your trading fund to begin with have between two to three thousand dollars. It is hard to make a great profit on any style of trading when you can only make a maximum of ten trades at one hundred dollars – this tied up the entire investment fund and it is quite likely that you will be making more than ten trades over the course of a single day through day trading. There are costs that need to be factored into your profit margins, mainly the cost of brokerage fees.

These fees will range on the brokerage firm that you use, but expect that they take around four percent of your total trade. For example, in day trading if I make a one-hundred-dollar investment, it's pretty normal to see a return of around twenty percent, or in this case twenty dollars. The brokerage fees would bring down my total profit to around sixteen dollars.

There is one piece of information I need to stress about your investment fund: you should only be using your investment fund for investments; it should not serve any other purpose. There are a plethora of reasons for this argument that I'm sure you already understand. In essence, this is legalized gambling, albeit based on concrete information that will give you a competitive advantage. Still, you never want to be using money that you might need to use to pay for rent or any other basic necessity. Also along these lines, I wouldn't use your retirement money for investing either. The reason beyond the obvious is that it limits your confidence in your trades.

You need to be willing to part with your money each and every time you make an investment. This frees you and your conscience on the investments that you make, and so you don't make knee jerk reactions to fluctuations in the market. If you think that you are going to use money for any other purpose, you are going to end up making some really poor decisions about when you should cash out. With the freedom of knowing that money is dedicated to investment, you will stick to your guns and stay invested where and when you need to.

CHAPTER 3

DAY TRADING

Day trading is my bread and butter, and its basis relies on making short term trades that typically you know the outcome of before the end of the trading day. The size of investment is typically between four to five hundred dollars for myself, and I will make around a dozen of these investments each and every day that I dedicate to day trading. If you are beginner, I would limit the size of your investments to around one hundred dollars, and your minimum should be at least eighty dollars. With a good trade, this would see your total profit for a one-hundred-dollar investment be around fifteen dollars. This might not sound a lot, but you will be making a lot of these trades each day.

Your path to profitability if you decide on day trading will be around three hundred dollars a week at first. Soon you will be able to get this up to five hundred and beyond, but a figure of around three hundred dollars a week to start is a good estimate for a beginner that is making intelligent trades and following the basic guidelines for how to make investments.

While a major selling point to day trading is that you don't need large amount of capital, there is a heavy time requirement. Day trading requires that you stay focused at your computer for six to ten hours. These six to ten hours are focused, and you will have little to no breaks to play games, converse with friends, run errands or focus on anything other than trading. Therefore, if you decide to focus on day trading, you need to ensure that you have an entire day to practice this one activity. In addition, you will need to schedule this time during the week. Since it is both time intensive and stress inducing, this style is not going to be a constant go to for a lot of traders. That being said, it is a style that you should practice at least a few times, and then perhaps stick to this style one or two days a week.

You can practice this style of trading on the weekends through aftermarket trading, but I really don't suggest that. The problem with trading on the weekend or after hours is that you are not presented with the key pieces of information that you need to make trades. Since the activity that you see is a reflection of only a small subset of trades, you get an incomplete picture of the market. This style of trading is extremely reliant on data based on what other traders are doing and any added limitations to this data will ultimately make your job much harder.

The basic strategy for day trading is focused on patterns. As a day trader, you don't' care about what a company sells or what product they are working on. You are going to be invested for such a short period of time that you simply don't have time to do research on what a company sells. The way that you will determine what to invest in is a function of looking for companies that have had relatively stable trends for two to three days. What you are looking for are stocks that have moved up and down in their total value of percentages of around fifteen to thirty percent. These are certainly major jumps but that is the type of volatility that you can expect in penny stocks. Chapter six will dive specifically into the type of volatility that you are looking for, but right now know that you are looking for stocks that have a lot of movement and have large market caps relative to the rest of the market.

Once you have identified a few companies that share these attributes, these being high volatility, relatively stable trends of increasing and decreasing stock value over a few days and sizeable market caps, you are ready to start investing. I like to find around a dozen of these companies. The problem is that there often doesn't exist a dozen of these types of perfect picks. What you will ultimately end of doing is expanding the parameters for what is an acceptable company to invest in. You will have some companies that only have volatility of ten or fifteen percent, and market caps that are not ideal. Of the total number of investments that I make in a day, I typically feel very comfortable with around three to four of them, are slightly skeptical with another three or four, and view the remainder as capital that I know I am going to invest, and am really not too sure about the ultimate pay off.

When I say that I am not too sure about the ultimate pay off, it means that I'm pretty confident I'm not going to lose money, but I'm not all that sure about how much profit I will really be able to make once I have paid all of the broker fees. It is still worth the investment because I know that I am dedicating my entire day to trading and so I will be sitting in front of my computer trading either way, but I know that these are not going to be my bread-winners for the week, and that the profits I can expect might only be returns of a little less than ten percent. Once you start making more sizable investments, returns of this percentage are still enough that it is completely worth making these investments, but early on I suggest you start with just three or four really solid picks.

That is because a huge part of being a successful day trader is not only making the right picks up front, but being able to cash out at exactly the right time. Let's do a quick example to show how a pick is made and run through the course of the day monitoring that trade and knowing exactly when to cash out.

Suppose that you find a company that meets your parameters for market capitalization and has had movements in volatility of around thirty percent for the last three or four days. This is a stock that I know I'm going to buy, but there is a question of what my goal post should be for when I should cash out. Since the basic strategy is that I am following the trend of the stock moving about thirty percent each day in a cycle, then I should ultimately feel comfortable with a twenty to twenty-five percent cash out point. That is, if I start my investment in the beginning of the day when the stock is at the lowest point for the last twenty-four hours, I tell myself that I am going to cash out near the twenty to twenty five percent mark. This is a key part of being consistently successful; if you do not create these limits for yourself, you end up holding onto a stock for too long and seeing the value decline while your money is still tied up.

As the stock starts to decline it becomes much harder to sell. For example, even though a stock might be trading for one dollar, if it is on its way down you won't be able to sell it for that price at that moment. Other traders are going to see that the price is heading in a downward trajectory and the total number of buy orders for that stock will plummet. This means that even though the current ticker value is at a dollar, it is unrealistic that you can clear all of the stock at this value. You might only be able to sell it at ninety-seven cents, and this three percent drop is going to eat very heavily into your profits. Therefore, the key here is to sell the stock on its way up and not when it hits the crest or starts to decline.

The crest of a stock provides the same problem as when the stock is heading downwards, only the problem isn't magnified as much. You will still have difficulty selling the stock because once the peak has been reached, the buy orders will start to dry up. You might be able to offload some of your stock at the ticker price, but it is doubtful that you will be able to offload all of the stock.

Take the example above of how I would conduct a single trade, and now imagine that you are doing this for twelve different companies. It becomes really easy to see how important constant monitoring is of the market. You will need to be truly present at your computer and watching the stock price of each and every pick that you have made for that day. The moment each one of your picks hits the prearranged value that you said you would sell the stock at, you make the sale. There are a couple of things that I want to note here: one, if the value of the stock goes far above the point where you sold the stock, you shouldn't feel bad that you missed out on an opportunity.

It can feel as though you are leaving money on the table, but the key to trading is not having a single big trade, but rather to trade consistently. If you kept your money in every stock for the entire duration that it was on the rise, you would ultimately be making far less money than cashing out while it is still on the way up. Again, you know when to cash out because you have seen that the trend for the stock is to move thirty percent in a day, therefore you want to sell the stock when it has moved twenty to twenty five percent; waiting till thirty percent ensures that you will have difficulty offloading all of your shares. The second thing to note is that while it might seem like an impossible task to monitor a dozen stocks at the same time, you do have some idea of how quickly these trends move based on past data. For example, you know that the stock moves thirty percent in a day, but you also have the last few days of trading data to know that the stock has cycles every two, four or six hours.

You can therefore focus on the stocks that have the shorter intervals in their trade values than the stocks that have a longer amount of time between hitting the highest point of their value. You will want to keep a steady eye on the stocks that modulate quickly and have in the background the stocks that modulate more slowly.

In summary, day traders act entirely on patterns and clear their books by the end of the day. They make a number of bets in the beginning of the trading day and sell that stock before the close of the markets. You will be making just a few trades each day when you start, somewhere around three to four, and each trade should max out at around one hundred dollars to start. You can expect returns of sixteen dollars per trade on each stock, which may seem small, but is completely adequate as you are testing the waters. You make your picks based on the market capitalization and the stocks that have high volatility and have moved in reliable patterns for the last two or three days. Most importantly, you sell the stock that you have before it starts to move in the downward direction.

You know when to sell on the way up because you plan to sell based on the past few days of data on the stock, agreeing that at a certain percentage of return you will make a sale. This is where most traders of penny stocks start off. Your competitive advantage in this trading style is going to be setting limits for your profitability. Remember, trading stock at it's peak value for that trading day, or even worse while it is on its way down, is a losing proposition. This is what most beginner traders do not understand and where they end up losing most of there money. If you stick within your limits, you will be on the wining side of every pick that you make.

CHAPTER 4

———

THE BUY AND HOLD STRATEGY

A buy and hold strategy is most commonly invoked when trading on traditional markets. In penny stocks, it is almost always a high-risk proposition. The basic premise is that you are looking at the detailed financials of a company and are betting that based on research about the future viability of that company. Companies tend to expand rather than contract if they are able to stay in business, and it is in this expansion where your profit is made. I have a few active trades that fall under the buy and hold strategy, and these are bets that I expect to be tied up in for many months, or even years.

The size of investment in a buy and hold strategy is among the largest of any common trading styles. You will want to bet the maximum amount per an individual trade in your investment fund, and it doesn't make sense to make an investment for less than around three to five thousand dollars. With these high requirements, and a long path to profitability, combined with the basic nature that companies that offer penny stocks typically aren't around for a long period of time, I can't recommend a buy and hold strategy to beginners. That being said, there exists a few strategies that you can invoke to increase your odds of success with this trading style. In addition, when this type of investment pays off, it pays off better than any other trading style.

An investment of three thousand dollars might pay off ten to twenty times that amount, and even that would be a relatively small profit margin for a penny stock that succeeds. The money and profit sound good, but you have to keep in mind the sizeable up front cost and the amount of time it takes to realize any profit at all.

Let's work with an example using a fictional company, Peach. For starters, you only want to adopt this style with companies that are trading on the New York Stock Exchange (NYSE). Chapter six will dive deeper into the different exchanges, but for right now know that the NYSE features penny stocks that are trading above one dollar, and are highly vetted in comparison to stocks that you will find on other penny stock exchanges. These are companies that might not go anywhere in the future, but at a bare minimum have had the type of vetting that would allow them to be listed on this prestigious exchange. With our fictional company, Peach, you would find this company listed on the sub section of the NYSE, under the value or penny stock section of the market. This is a section that is removed from the more traditional companies that you might be familiar with, like J.P. Morgan and McDonald's.

Your decision to invest in Peach is based on extensive research on the company and that you truly believe in their product. For our example, let's say that Peach offers a type of social network where the users own their own data. The reason that this might seem like an attractive proposition is because a main complaint of the largest social network, Facebook, is over the way that they handle privacy and the fact that they own the data of all of their users. If Peach were to see even moderate success, it could increase in value many dozens of times over. It is not enough however that you believe in the underlying product that Peach is trying to create, you need to know much more beyond this.

You need to have detailed information about their CEO, their business model moving forward, their current assets, how far along they are to publishing their product and much more. How you get this information is also important, as a key rule of penny stock companies is that you cannot trust the company line. Companies are desperate for investment, and they will often cut corners where they can, lying about how far they are along product development or faking financial reports altogether. The fact that you have selected a stock on the NYSE mitigates this somewhat, but you will still need to do your research before you make an investment.

You may be wondering how you could be privy to such information. The answer is quite simple; the investment you are going to make is sizable, and three thousand dollars to a penny stock company is enough that you can request all the information you need. They absolutely will provide it to you if you are clear about your intentions with the company. They love the idea of a long-term investor that is willing to support them with a sizeable investment and is not going to sell their shares for months or years. They will bend over backwards to make sure that you make this investment because they know that this is a long-term bet for you. The next part is difficult, and requires a bit of knowledge about the sector of the economy that you are investing in. When you look over the information that the company has provided, you really need to understand the documentation of both the financials and underlying product.

The company in this example is a social media competitor to Facebook. The type of requisite knowledge that you need to have is more than just understanding that people would love to own their own data. You need to be aware of the current business model that Facebook uses, as well as all of the up and coming competitors to

Facebook and the business models that Facebook's competitors are seeking. All of this means that the best way to practice buy and hold trading is to only invoke this strategy in sectors of the economy that you have a distinct familiarity with. I would never invest in the fictional company Peach because my basic understanding of how social media companies operate is not as detailed as it would need to be to make the best investments. The more specific your knowledge and the sector of the economy that it describes, the more this type of investment will start to make sense. This is not necessary a high-level strategy, but the amount of knowledge you need coupled with the very high capital requirements for penny stock trading make it a strategy that you should only invoke once you have made a decent amount of profit trading on the other trading styles that I describe. For my part, the two large investments that I have made as part of a buy and hold strategy were made from profits garnered through day trading and value trading. I would suggest that you adopt this as well, and only attempt a buy and hold strategy with the profits that you have made from other styles of trading.

There are a few other details of buy and hold trading that are worth mentioning. For this style, the market capitalization of a company does not really matter; neither does the volatility beyond a certain point. You are betting on an idea and the people that are supporting that idea, and the metrics on which that company operates today are going to be far different from where it is operating in just a few years. The last detail I must mention is that unlike other trading styles, the length of such an investment means that you could suffer a one hundred percent loss when invoking this style. On traditional exchanges, and in FOREX markets, there is little chance that the value of a commodity drops to zero. Big companies might get decimated, but they will at least retain *some* value due to the assets that they hold.

Starbucks for example, even if a terrible fate were to bestow them, their retail stores that are owned by corporate would still exist. As such, these retail stores could always be sold to reimburse stockholders to some degree. The same cannot be said with penny stock companies that do not have that many assets, and are often times operating under a decent amount of debt. The three-thousand-dollar investment in Peach could therefore theoretically drop to zero in a way that simply could not happen with a larger company. The ultimate lesson that you should walk away with from a buy and hold strategy is that while it is risky and you could potentially lose your whole investment, if you have enough confidence in a product or service and the people trying to bring it to market, it might be worth making the investment.

CHAPTER 5

VALUE TRADING

After day trading, value trading is the style that you are most likely to invoke for at least some of your investment portfolio. The basic premise to value trading is more complicated than with day trading and the buy and hold strategy. It combines understanding the market capitalization of a company with researching the assets that a company holds. In the world of penny stocks, there are only so many companies that satisfy the requirements to be reasonable investments for value trading, but if you can follow the advice I have, it also offers the highest degree of success.

The basic premise of value trading is that you are investing in a company because you are seeing something other investors are not, assets or ideas that could be patented that raise the value of the company's stock above its current value. To explain this idea, let's take an unlikely scenario that could befall McDonald's. McDonald's is a good stock for long term investment and their stock price has remained stable over the years, increasing and decreasing accordingly with the market, but has not been subject to all of the rapid changes in the economy. For example, after the 2008 financial crisis, McDonald's stock would prove to be among one of the most resilient on major exchanges due to the demand for their products remaining stable regardless of the state of the economy as a whole.

Suppose for a moment that some terrible news were to come out about McDonald's, news that would send the stock price to the absolute lowest value you could imagine. For the purposes of this example, we are going to make that value a single cent. If McDonald's were trading at this very low value after a terrible news story, would it make sense to buy that the stock? The answer is, yes, absolutely. Only a fool wouldn't buy McDonald's stock at one cent. Now this might be obvious to you too, but the reasons for why this is a safe investment are probably very different. You might believe that their stock will increase because after the news story has faded away, customers would return to their store and their business would return to normal.

Suppose that the news story was a permanent decrease in the number of customers they could attract, and that they would never be able to recover. Even if McDonald's never sold another hamburger it would still be a wise investment when the stock is trading at one cent. It makes sense to buy McDonald's stock because the stock price does not accurately reflect the real assets that McDonald's owns.

McDonald's is a chain restaurant that has franchised the name and products that it serves. McDonalds across the country and the world are owned independently, but the McDonald's corporation owns some number of those stores themselves. If the stock price of McDonald's were trading at one cent, think about what that means for the total value of the company as a whole. We can see the total value based on the market capitalization. In this case, that market cap would be a relatively low number to what it was before, but if McDonald's were to sell all of the land on which it has build its many restaurants, it would certainly be more than the market capitalization when the stock is trading at one cent. This incongruity between the market cap and the total cost of all of the assets that McDonald's holds means that the stock price *has* to increase.

It simply is a clerical error that the stock price could fall to a number so low. The lesson here is that when the market cap doesn't match the total number of assets, there needs to be a course correct. It is worth mentioning that this isn't true if the market cap is greater than the total number of assets, but only when the market cap is lower than the total number of assets. This can be a confusing concept because it works in one direction, but does not prove to be true in the opposite. The reason why this is true is because when the market cap is greater than the sum of all of the assets of a company, it represents the degree of faith that investors have about the potential future of the company. This makes up for the discrepancy in why the market cap is greater than the sum of the assets.

In the opposite direction, when the market cap is lower than the assets, it needs to course correct because selling all of the assets would be a sum greater than the market cap. In our example, all McDonald's would need to do is sell all of the land on which it owns stores and suddenly they would have more money on hand than their market cap. Investors will soon realize this and the stock price would increase. In the case of the horrible news story that destroys the future profitability of McDonald's, investors would still flock back because the stock price will increase as McDonald's sells all of the land that it owns.

How this works with penny stocks is a little bit different than how it works with larger established companies. Remember that penny stock companies typically don't have many assets and are often operating in debt. The assets that an investor needs to be on the lookout for are ideas that could be sold to corporations at a later date. Let's illustrate this using another example with a fictional penny stock company, Strawberry. Strawberry is a tech company built around compression software. They have created a way to compress data more efficiently than any major software company on the market. They are however a small company, and are operating in debt. The likelihood that Strawberry will exist long into the future is low, however they are sitting on some amazing technology. Before Strawberry fades away, it would be wise for them to sell the technology that they have developed. They could either sell this technology directly to another company, or they could sell it in the form of a patent. It is very difficult to quantity what the value of Strawberry's technology is worth, but suppose for a moment that the company's current market cap was just over three million dollars. The technology that they have is obviously worth far more than that. Similarly, to the incongruity between the market cap and the value of the total assets for McDonald's, the value of Strawberry's stock is destined to rise. Just like McDonald's, they might completely fade away into existence, but before that happens their stock value will at least match the value of the technology as they sell the idea to another company.

How you are expected to find hidden value in companies is not easy, but it is not as difficult as you might think either. I have made a decent amount of money from this style of trading, and the key is to work within sectors of the economy that you are familiar with. I personally have had more success working with companies that trade on the NYSE, but there is no reason why you cannot find solid value companies on smaller exchanges as well. The primary asset that you are looking for are ideas that can be sold to other companies; these mainly arise in the form of patents. The best way for you to discover if a company is close to patenting an idea, or if they have an idea that is likely to be of value in the future, is to reach out to that company start a dialogue.

This is the key similarity between this trading style and a buy and hold approach to trading. Just like with buy and hold trading, you do have to be aware that companies are desperate for investment and will try very hard to sell you on the idea of investment. This is why you need some background knowledge in the field that the company operates, so you are at least able to determine if what they are working on is a real and viable idea that can be sold to a larger company.

The next step after you have found a company that has an idea that might be of value, but currently has no path to market by themselves, is to look at their total asset list and the amount of debt that they owe. You can partly do this by merely glancing at the market capitalization to see what the extent of the total amount of loans that they can take out. A greater market cap indicates a company that has a higher degree of success for being able to sell its idea. This is simply because they have more room for that idea to grow and to finalize and patent the idea before it is sold. The market capitalization does not tell you everything you need to know though. You will also need to do more detailed research into the company to determine their total liabilities, which can often extend far beyond the market capitalization. To fully explain this idea, let's have another look at Strawberry and how their liabilities far outweigh their ability to sell their technology.

At this point, you have conducted your initial research into Strawberry and believe that their compression technology is worth more than their market capitalization. This only tells part of the story however, and you need to account for the long list of possible liabilities that the company might be indebted for. For example, just last year I lost money on an investment because I did not do enough research into the owners of a company creating a new type of simple shipping container. The basic premise of the product was that it would be a one size fits all shipping container for non-commercial use. The cost of the container was very cheap and could fit all sorts of items. I still think it was a good idea, and I believe the patent on that idea would have been worth a few million dollars to someone like FedEx or UPS.

The problem was that one of the inventors was in the middle of a bitter lawsuit between relatives and himself over the inheritance from an estranged family member. He was using company resources to pay for lawyer fees for years, and the market cap of the company did not reflect that the owner had sewed so much of the company's on hand cash in this bitter feud. For the part of Strawberry, something quite similar could happen. You might wonder how an individual could abuse the financial resources of a company like this, and the answer is that these companies are so small that these types of abuses are not only possible, they're quite prevalent. Penny stock companies are so small that owners typically use the financial backing of these companies to pay for rent, food and other expenses.

This is actually a minor issue with penny stocks, and not something you should be particularly concerned about. As an investor, I don't actually mind if the research and development team is living off of borrowed money backed by the investments in the penny stock; it allows for the research and development in the first place. It only becomes a problem when the total cost of liabilities starts to outweigh the market cap. Rent, food and other necessities can't do this, but something like a long-lasting lawsuit, that's a different story.

There are other liabilities that you have to be aware of as well. On the part of Strawberry, suppose that the software for data compression caused computers to run as very high temperatures, and made them likely to start a fire. I know this is not an actual possibility, but I'm using this to demonstrate a large liability that undermines the value of the patent on the data compression technology. Suddenly what could be a multi-million-dollar patent is weighed down by the cost of what it would be to fix all of the computers destroyed by that very software. It is then your role as an investor to research these companies, the products and people behind them, and ensure that there are no outstanding legal obligations or issues that could arise down the road that undermines how valuable the sellable idea is.

In summary, value traders focus on finding value in a company that is not present in the current market capitalization. In the case of Strawberry, the idea of data compression is worth far more than the market cap because the cost of an outside company selling the patent is far more than the cost of all outstanding shares multiplied by the average share price. This type of trading is conducive to those that don't have the time for rigid block schedules required for day trading. Research can be done on your own time and be conducted over the course of several weeks or months. You will want to make fairly large investments when you do find that companies that offer an idea or have assets are worth more than their market cap.

Investments that tend be truly profitable require around one thousand dollars at a minimum, although this does not mean that you should go above the ten percent per single investment rule. You would therefore ideally have an investment fund of ten thousand dollars to make this style of trade regularly. Of all of the styles of trading, I find that this is the safest. It is a basic principle that the stock price will rise if the assets of a company are greater than the market cap. Use this basic rule to make profit as the stock rises when the assets are sold off, either material assets or ideas that can be patented and sold to larger companies.

CHAPTER 6

LIQUIDITY, VOLATILITY AND UNDERSTANDING THE EXCHANGES

Why Liquidity Matters

In the world of penny stocks, liquidity is one of the key determining factors in whether or not you should be buying stock. Liquidity is your ability to sell stock and is a function of the *spread*. Liquidity is important in all markets, but when it comes to penny stocks, the margins on profits can be destroyed by poor liquidity. Thankfully it is quite easy to determine the liquidity of a penny stock, and depending on the type of trading style that you adopt, it will have more or less importance accordingly. For your purposes, you should pay the most attention to liquidity when day trading. It is those split-second changes in your ability to offload stock that will greatly modify your ability to move shares.

Liquidity is determined by the spread of a stock. If you are new to investing, the spread is the difference between the bid price and ask price of a stock. For example, suppose that you wanted to buy one hundred shares of Dunkin Donut's stock. If the stock is currently trading at fifty dollars, the actual cost to you is going to be slightly more. Part of this cost is the brokerage fee, but even if we ignore this cost, there is still going to be a difference between the ask price and the theoretical bid price of fifty dollars. The ask price is what sellers of the stock are currently requesting for the stock. When you are buying stock directly from the company, the ask price tends to be relatively stable to the indexed price, in this case the ticker price of fifty dollars.

However, most of the time you are not buying stock directly from the issuing company, but rather you are purchasing shares from other trades that are trying to offload their own holdings. While the ticker price might indicate fifty dollars, this is just the most recent sale as it has been updated. Depending on the exchange that you are working with, the refresh rate for this number could be several seconds, or it could be a couple of minutes. This time differential is large enough that the effective sale price is never the same as the ticker price. If a trader were trying to offload one hundred shares, the same number you want to buy, their ask price might be $50.25. Since the ticker price was shown to be fifty dollars, this is your effective bid price. The spread therefore is the difference between these two numbers, or twenty-five cents. The larger the spread of the stock price, the more difficulty you will have offloading stock. Notice that either the buyer or the seller of the stock in question needs to budge on the price for a sale to be made. The larger the spread becomes, the harder the stock is to move.

In preceding chapters, you learned about the different trading styles that you will be using for penny stocks. The trading style that requires immediate sale of a stock to make a keen profit is day trading. This is where the spread is going to matter the most. As a typical rule, the larger the market cap for a company, the tighter the spread will be on average. Although this does not dictate the spread will be tight at any given moment, you can generally bet that you will be able to offload the stock with little issue.

Penny stocks are unique in how wide the spread can sometimes be. Some penny stock companies, particular those not located on the NYSE, will have such wide spreads that it is effectively impossible to sell the stock, no matter what you set the ask price to. This is because many of the companies can fold very quickly. For day trading, when you are making your initial purchase of stock, you will want to have a tight spread and market caps of over two million dollars. I gave a strong word of advice that you need to sell the stock that you are holding as it is increasing in value. This is because the spread of the stock so greatly increases once the stock reaches its peak value in that trading cycle, and will get wider as the stock price starts to decrease. By selling the stock on its way up, you avoid the problem of a wide spread cutting into your profits. Essentially, the ticker price will be more representative of what you are able to sell the stock for as it is increasing in value, and will become less reliable as the stock starts to decrease in value.

For other trading styles the spread is not nearly as helpful for determining the ultimate liquidity of a stock. That is because the spread is only useful in the very short term, and other trading styles are longer investments that are weeks, months, and in some cases, years. My suggestion is that if you are using any trading style outside of day trading, that you focus on companies that have a market cap above one million dollars. The minimum market cap that I suggest you invest into needs to be above five hundred thousand; anything lower, and I think it is a very risky proposition that you will be able to sell the stock in the future. There is no hard-fast rule to this, and these are merely guidelines, but the last few years have shown me that this a great way of ensuring that I can generally offload stock for longer term investments in companies.

When Volatility Matters

A key advantage to penny stocks is the high volatility that you will find in the marketplace. Volatility is measured in the percentage change that a company's stock regularly undergoes. For day trading, you know that the percentage change that you are looking for should be around thirty percent. These types of swings are the ideal percentage to look for, and more specifically you are looking for those types of changes that occur over a period of six to eight hours. On any given day, you should be able to find three to four stocks that have changes of thirty percent or greater, and these changes can be found as repeatable patterns over the last two to three days of trading. The minimum level of volatility that you should be looking for in day trading is ten percent. Volatility that is lower than this amount is not worth investing in due to the fees of from your broker.

For other trading styles, volatility will matter far less but it still does play a role. You can think of volatility as activity on a stock, and low or no volatility means a company that is stagnant and you will always have a hard time moving shares. That being said, the other strategies rely on longer time frames, so as long as there are changes of five to ten percent over the course of a week, that is acceptable for investment, provided that these picks also have the other characteristics mentioned from the previous chapters, such as having a market cap minimum of half a million dollars.

Understanding the Exchanges That Handle Penny Stocks

There are two primary exchanges on which you should be trading penny stocks, the Over the Counter Bulletin Board (OTCBB) and the NYSE. There are other places where you will find penny stocks being traded, but these other exchanges have such poor minimum standards of what stocks they list that is simply not worth the effort of doing trades. This is not advice that is universal, and I've read plenty of counter arguments for why other exchanges are fine for day trading, but I'm a staunch believer that plenty of profit can be made from the OTCBB and NYSE. The function of these exchanges is to house all of the companies trading within them and to link directly to brokerage houses where you will be trading stock.

The NYSE has a smaller exchange that sells only penny stocks. These companies actually trade at values typically over one dollar. The NYSE costs a premium to trade on, but what you are paying for that premium is the ability to trade on companies that are fairly well vetted. It historically has been a problem in the penny stock community that companies will inaccurately list their total assets, and lie about how far along development on services or products they are. This fraud has ranged from minor inaccuracies, to widespread lies about how far along a company is in research and development, or whether or not they are able to accomplish the goals that they have claimed to already have accomplished. The NYSE does a good job of vetting companies to be listed on the exchange. This vetting process is in combination with the SEC, which will look over some documentation to ensure that companies are truthful in their holdings, liabilities and the essential information to know if a company will be around for a long time. As such, the premium that you pay on these companies should be used for making investments in the strategies of buy and hold and value trading. For me personally, I pretty much exclusively practice value trading on the NYSE. It is simply easier to look through documentation to ensure that asset lists are correct and a company is indeed producing a real product or service. You can practice day trading on the NYSE, but expect the total volatility to be lower than what you will find on the OTCBB.

The OTCBB is the best place for day trading. The main issue with other exchanges is that they don't have the network infrastructure to conduct trades as quickly as is necessary to offload and make purchases at the right spreads. The OTCBB will be the exchange where you conduct most of your trades in the beginning as you focus on day trading. Day trading allows for trades that do not need to be too sizeable by themself, plus you will be able to cash out each day. The OTCBB offers some degree of vetting for stocks, but nowhere near the same degree as what you can expect on the NYSE. To find the stocks that have the most volatility on the OTCBB, you will simply have to refer to your broker's tools and the index of the most active stocks. It is a simple enough process that just requires you have some practice with your broker's tools. You should find that within a couple of hours of experimenting on your broker's website, that you should have the requisite knowledge to find your way around and pick the stocks with suitable volatility.

CHAPTER 7

KEY STRATEGIES & ADVICE FOR SMARTER INVESTING

Don't Trust the Company Line

Remember that companies are desperate for investment. When it comes to the buy and hold and value trading strategies, assume that any piece of documentation has some degree of hyperbole to facts and figures. This won't be so much of an issue for day trading, but for any investment that you are making for longer than a week, you will want to be sure that you are at least investing in what you think is a good product or idea. This is especially true if you communicate with a company and believe that they are on their way to patenting an idea. I have had on several occasions found out through further inquiry that a technology was so far away from becoming a patentable idea that the company simply wasn't worth the investment. Be vigilant and you will find there are a few gems out there that are worth in investing in; you just have to sort through the rubbish.

Try Different Trading Styles, but Focus First on Day Trading

Buy and hold trading and value trading require research and sizeable investments to make decent returns. I am firm believer that you should eventually try all styles of investment, but realistically the one that you will be making the most money from at first is day trading. It requires the least amount of knowledge about any sector of the economy and requires you to make enough trades that you familiarize yourself with the OTCBB and the NYSE. It should only take around one to two months before you are looking at the value of stock and are able to figure in the cost of broker fees automatically; this will allow you to make trades more efficiently as you won't have to calculate your profitability on a separate document. You will be able to see the volatility and trade volume and be able to make an accurate prediction to how much money you will make on a single trade. This is an important skill to have with day trading where every minute counts.

Keep a Trade Log

Perhaps the most important piece of advice that I can give you is that you should keep a trade log with every single trade that you make. This logbook should house all trades no matter how big or small, and needs to include all of the information pertinent to each trade. This includes information like the buy and sale price of the trade, the cost of broker fees, date of the trade, the strategy that you were basing the trade on, and most importantly, *why* you made that specific trade. The only way to truly get better at trading under any strategy is to analyze your past trades. Without this, you are doomed to make the same mistakes over and over gain. Even if a majority of your trades are successful, you want to reduce the number of mistakes that you make regardless. I have become a much better trader over time because of a trade log. It does not matter if this is a physical note-book or if it is a long form Google document, just keep a trade log and refer to it once a week. Review your trades and analyze what went right and what went wrong.

For example, before I started trading I thought that I would mainly focus on being a value trader. What I ulti-mately discovered through the aid of my trade log was that the dollar to profit ratio on day trading was much higher than what I was making through all of the research involved in value trading. This is the type of insight that a trade log can offer you, invaluable information that is just on the periphery. Trust me, you won't be able to get a true sense for your competitive advantage unless you keep a trade log. It is a time-consuming affair but is cer-tainly worth the effort in terms of the increased profits that you will make as you identify your strengths and weaknesses.

Practice Trading Before Any Real Investment

Before you invest a single dollar in any stock, I highly suggest that you practice for one to two weeks with your trade log. This primarily works with day trading above the other styles of investing due to the time scale of investment. You should use a trade log and make pretend trades based on real data. This will give you an idea about the type of return on investment that you can expect to see. To mimic the type of impact that broker fees will have on your profits, simply factor in a four percent surcharge for all of your purchases and sales. Even if you are not going to dedicate a full day to trading, you can at least look at a variety of stocks and see when the ideal times are to buy and stock and when to sell. This will give you a general idea to the trends of stocks and how they modulate throughout the day. You should also be realistic about the size of the investment that you are working with, betting at most ten percent of your total investment dollars in any one stock. This will give you an accurate picture of the type of returns that you will be able to garner over the first few weeks of trading.

Don't Pay for Advanced Brokerage Tools

I decided not to include a section in this book about what brokerage firm you should use for investing. This is because the rates that brokers charge is going to be relative to how much money you deposit in your account at any firm. Realistically for starting investors you are best off using whoever has the cheapest rates as all other factors are not nearly as important. For beginners, *Scottrade* is a decent firm to use, as their rates are relatively modest and their interface is relatively easy to use. The one detail I want to stress to you is that you should never pay extra fees to use advanced analyst tools. These tools simply aren't worth the dent that they create in your profitability on individual trades.

The main difference between tools from different brokers is not in the data that they present to you, but rather the ease of use of sorting through this data. Any firm that you decide to trade with however, you will become accustomed to their tools after just a few trades. Use what's cheapest and then become aquatinted with the tools. When you're trading with low amounts of capital, you will need the lowest fees to make profit figures that are worth your time and effort.

You Can Make Money Even During a Pump and Dump Scheme

The number one threat to penny stocks is that fraud can be more rampant than you might find on traditional stock exchanges. Even though this is a basic truth of penny stocks, the main type of large scale fraud, the pump and dump scheme, can still gain profit for traders that get in early and are not too greedy with the amount of profit that they seek. The way that a pump and dump scheme works is a public facing figure, typically a celebrity, will promote a penny stock. They might claim that they are getting involved in the penny stock, which seems to be the most common way that this scheme unfolds. Investors believing that the stock is sure to reach mass market because of the fact that a celebrity is getting involved, will then invest in the stock, driving up the value.

Before the public facing figure announces to the world that they are investing in the stock, they would have already purchased many shares of that stock at the cheapest possible price. They stand to make a great deal of money by pumping up the stock with the investment from outside investors and those that hear about the celebrity's involvement. The stock then suddenly plummets when the main investor, the celebrity themself, sells their shares. This sets off a chain reaction as all other investors start to feel that the stock is no longer a sure-fire bet to reach the mass market.

At first glance it might appear that a stock that is being propped up by a celebrity is something that you should avoid wholesale, but the truth is a little bit more complicated than that. There are plenty of investors that make a decent amount of profit from pump and dump schemes outside of the celebrity figure that propped up the stock. The key is that they got involved at the right time, realized the scheme for what it was, and then cashed out before the stock started to fall. To make this work you have to realize what is going on when a stock like this goes through the roof. The most recent example of this happened just a few years ago with rapper Fifty Cent. He promoted an import company and saw the stock multiply many times over. Investors believed that this company would be able to make it onto the major exchanges and that it would eventually hit a share price of twenty or even thirty dollars.

The truth was that this was just a pump and dump scheme and that Fifty Cent would soon sell his shares. He ultimately ended up making millions, but there were plenty of regular investors that that walked away with hundreds of thousands of dollars as well. They sold the stock after they had made some profit, but well before Fifty Cent sold his stock. When the celebrity figure sells his or her stock, since they own such a large percentage of the outstanding shares, the stock will suddenly go into a free fall. The stock price could plummet in a matter of days, if not hours. The only way to get ahead of this is to sell the stock before the public facing figure dumps their shares.

Investors that were greedy and continued to watch the stock rise ultimately did not make as much money. Even though they participated for a longer amount of time and saw the stock rise in value far above when other traders started to sell, you now understand the concept of the spread widening when a stock hits its crest and starts to fall. It was a race to the bottom and anyone that stuck around after Fifty Cent sold his shares either lost out on potential profits, or flat out lost same of their base investment.

The odds of another major pump and dump scheme happening are slim. This most recent occurrence with Fifty Cent pushed the SEC to make much stricter regulations on penny stocks to avoid this type of scenario from happening again. Realistically, it will happen again in the future, but on a slightly smaller scale. The type of public facing figure that would participate in such a scheme is also likely to not be a person but rather an investment firm that gets involved in a penny stock not out of malice, but to actually make a legitimate investment. Once the public has become aware that an investment firm of even a medium size has become involved in a penny stock, you can expect a similar pattern to follow.

There is an inherent risk in investing in a stock that is being propped up by a single entity through a pump and dump scheme, but it has been shown in the past that plenty of investors can still make money if they get invested for just a short period of time. For myself, if such an event were to occur in the future, I would certainly still invest in the penny stock company and wait for the stock to rise ten or fifteen percent before I sell the stock. I would treat it like a minor day trading pick and not like a major cash cow. I would also keep my investment to a relatively modest amount, perhaps around five to eight hundred dollars.

CONCLUSION

Thank you again for downloading *Penny Stocks: The Beginner's Guide to Building Massive Wealth.*

You now have the essential knowledge you need to start trading and making money through penny stocks. Your first step is to create a trade log and to do a week of practice before you start investing with your own money. This will allow you to test the waters and see how the market capitalization and volatility of a stock impacts your ability to buy and sell close to the ticker price. This is an optional step, but one that I ultimately think that you should take. After your week of practice, I suggest that you start with day trading as your primary strategy. This is the best place to start for beginners, and while your total profits will not be very large to start with, they will be proportional to the size of your investment fund. Remember that each investment should be between five and ten percent of your total fund, and that investments larger than this come with added risks that could impact the success you have on your other trades. You know what to look for when it comes to day trading, and to make it easier on yourself, start with just three or four trades each day. You will need to schedule dedicated blocks of time for trading, time when you will be able to focus your entire attention on monitoring your investments and cashing out at the right time.

I can't stress enough that your success as a penny stock trader is dependent on your ability to keep an accurate trade log of every investment that you make. Regardless of the strategy that you adopt, a trade log is paramount to identifying your strengths and weaknesses in trading. This point of reflection is where a lot of traders stumble, and without looking back on your past performance, it will be difficult to improve your profitability in the future.

As you progress with day trading, you must note that not every single day is going to be profitable. This is true with every investor, no matter how successful. The key is to have more successful days than unsuccessful ones.

If you follow the guidance I offer, I am sure that you will be able to make decent profit. Don't be too greedy and remember to cash out on individual trades as the stock is moving upward. You know that the spread will widen as the price on a stock hits its maximum value for that trading cycle. You need to sell your holdings before this point to make the greatest level of profit; the ticker price only tells part of the story, and does not accurately reflect the price at which you will be able to offload all of your stock. This is a major mistake that many traders make early on. If you can create your limits and know when to sell stock in the trading cycle, you will be at a significant advantage.

Lastly if you enjoyed this book, it would be much appreciated if you could leave a review. The best way for this book to make its way into the hands of more readers is through truthful reviews about this work. Please write what you liked about this book and what could be improved upon. Any and all feedback is helpful as I continue to serve the needs of my readership.

Thank you and good luck!

www.ingramcontent.com/pod-product-compliance
Lightning Source LLC
Chambersburg PA
CBHW071226220526
45468CB00002B/752